Blood & Cord: Writers on

"Many kinds of parenthood are p
new collection of poems and stories. Mothers and
fathers convey the spectrum of ways in which the self
is remade by parenthood, the 'complete subjugation'
of this task – bodily, mentally, spiritually – tearing
apart the boundaries of love for which new language
is required. Thankfully, the writers herein are more
than up to this otherwise monumental task. New and
experienced parents alike will find solace and resonance
in this wonderful book." – Carolyn Jess-Cooke

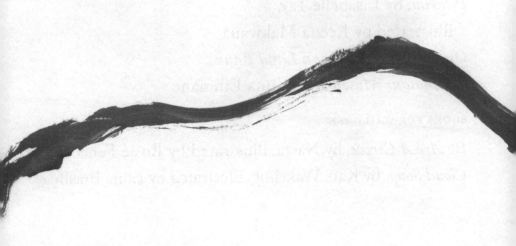

OTHER TITLES FROM THE EMMA PRESS

SHORT STORIES AND ESSAYS

How Kyoto Breaks Your Heart, by Florentyna Leow
Night-time Stories, edited by Yen-Yen Lu
Hailman, by Leanne Radojkovich
Postcard Stories 2, by Jan Carson
Tiny Moons: A year of eating in Shanghai,
  by Nina Mingya Powles

POETRY COLLECTIONS

Europe, Love Me Back, by Rakhshan Rizwan

POETRY AND ART SQUARES

The Strange Egg, by Kirstie Millar,
  illustrated by Hannah Mumby
The Fox's Wedding, by Rebecca Hurst,
  illustrated by Reena Makwana
Pilgrim, by Lisabelle Tay,
  illustrated by Reena Makwana
*One day at the Taiwan Land Bank
  Dinosaur Museum,* by Elīna Eihmane

BOOKS FOR CHILDREN

We Are A Circus, by Nasta, illustrated by Rosie Fencott
Cloud Soup, by Kate Wakeling, illustrated by Elīna Brasliņa

INTRODUCTION
FROM THE EDITOR

The birth of a baby is like a comet crashing into your living room, like a door inside yourself opening up, like being inside a tempest. Becoming a new parent is one of life's greatest joys, and much of what we read and see on social media and in popular culture tells us so: blooming mothers flushed with love, adoring, doting fathers, proud grandparents. But there is an unedited side to the story: it is also full of other emotions, some of them ambivalent, and this storm of emotions is often under-portrayed. Becoming a parent can be a kind of un-making of the self. You lose your old life in many ways, both physically and emotionally. From the intensity of birth, to the strange hinterlands of sleepless nights, from the pain of baby loss, to the ferocity of love, to the sensation of having allowed a being into your world who will change it forever.

The remade version of the parent has undergone a profound transformation. The writers in this collection, some fathers, some mothers, explore this territory with searing honesty and originality. The introduction of a new baby rearranges a life, and this requires a new language and a new kind of engagement with the world. The fictions, memoirs and poetry within these pages will illuminate parenthood in unexpected ways. The title, *Blood & Cord*, is taken from a beautiful poem by Gail McConnell, 'Talk Through the Wall', which explores a form of parenthood where both parents are women, and the speaker of the poem seeks to situate herself as the partner who is not pregnant. This exemplifies how the anthology aims to represent many possible versions of parenthood. The writers here are already known and admired for their writing on parenthood, and with brand new work and work collected from award-winning volumes, they will move, surprise and console new parents everywhere.

ABI CURTIS, 2023

CONTENTS

NAOMI BOOTH

What is tsunami? 1

GAIL MCCONNELL

Talk Through the Wall 10

Now 12

Untitled / Villanelle 14

An Apple Seed 16

MALCOLM TAYLOR

To be where I am not 19

LIZ BERRY

The Other Mothers 21

Godspeed 23

Princes End 25

Blue Heaven 27

RACHEL BOWER

Flight 29

Continue on Loop 31

Ruth Charnock

three tarot cards for the new mother 33

Abi Curtis

September Birth 50

Ultrasound 52

On my son, falling asleep 55

Water Birth 56

Jennifer Cooke

Inside the Eye 58

Paige Davis

This Too Will Pass 64

Janine Bradbury

Meridian 66

Stranger Days 67

Jellyfish 68

Elizabeth Hogarth

Animal Body 69

Shark Tooth 71

Injured Bird 72

SYLVIE SIMONDS

The bonds of love 74

ALEX MCRAE DIMSDALE

Bath 75
Disaster 78
Feeding the Baby 80
Things I have removed from my baby's mouth . . . 82
Covenant 84

DAISY HILDYARD

Waste 86

REBECCA GOSS

Other Mothers 94

CALEB KLACES

The Carrier Bag Theory of Fiction 104

SANDRA SIMONDS

Bikram Yoga 110
Lace Clouds over House over House over House . . . 112
Exploding Florida 114

Tommy Brad

Expectant father 116

Author biographies *118*

Permissions *126*

About The Emma Press *128*

Also from The Emma Press *129*

Naomi Booth

What is tsunami?

In the beginning, there were no words. You lay back in
the hospital bed, stunned. The midwife went about her
business in the background. There were low murmurs
in the corridor beyond you. Cries torn from other
women, at the dark peak of their own labours. And
here, handed onto your chest, flesh incarnate: silent,
waxy lozenge of an infant.

There were no words as the baby slept, hot and larval,
in the plastic box beside you. The ward was empty,
except for the two of you. Your own small movements
– tentative steps towards the bathroom, which brought
fresh blood, the rearrangement of the baby's blanket –
were muffled and sacred.

No words, on that first night when they let you take
the baby home and you lay her down beside you in the
bassinet. Of course not. What were you expecting?

An infant who exited the womb trilling with speech? Of course not. But still, it was unnerving. This absence of language. In those first nights, deep in the winter, when you swaddled her and tried to teach her to sleep, and you listened through the quiet hours to the bizarre, guttural sounds that came as she cleared her throat and lungs.

No one had told you that an early baby is less like something new, and more like something ancient and broken. Dark-sea fish, dredged from the Midnight Zone, sputtering water. Cawing pterodactyl of a baby.

The baby feeds incessantly through those long nights. The baby feeds and feeds and she rockets up the percentiles for weight. Her arms and legs uncoil and her belly fattens and she no longer looks like an injured relic. Her body writhes with the desire to move. She wants to be near to you, always. She mewls when anyone else holds her. The baby's father grows angry at his redundancy. Then he is elsewhere.

The baby learns to focus her eyes on you – and there is an ardency in her gaze then that makes you think of locked-in syndrome.

When the baby first laughs it is a bleat. It is a hard burst of joy fired out into the world, surprising you both, and it finally breaks your fear of her.

Then she is singing to you. Before she can speak, she babbles in long, tuneful patterns – la da da da da la la la, ma ma ma ma, da da da, ow wow ow wow bow wow wow, row row row, uh-ooh uh-ooh uh-ooh uh-ooh – her frequent song of accidents – which will make it impossible for you to remember her first words, because they emerge and recede, emerge and recede, back and forth in a wash of sound, until one day she is saying quite distinctly to you, pointing to your plate, Mama, Mama, Isla eat, and you are elated at the ring of her voice, sweet and forceful, and you are sorrowful too at the loss of her peculiar sonar.

Still, she makes these new words her own: I got the chicken pops. Baby is mines. I live on planet erf.

The cow is milking out some drink for its baby. Oh, it's breezing. The sky is winding again. That's the porcupine tree. What if there's none breakfast? Let's cook it in the hotenator. You're a naughty clogs. I will do it NONE ways. Stop tickling – I'll be egg-scrambled. It's the earringest day. Pretend I'm a little girl that's got none eyes. Morer. Do it to infinity. Persons shouldn't run on roads. This day is it Monday? On the threeth time, I'll stop. I am desperately Santa. I'm save-the-daying.

She names her favourite doll, Hearty Campfire. She names her favourite rabbit, Cunt. Or sometimes, Cunty-wunty.

You do not correct her speech. You longed for a shared language, and then you find that you cannot initiate her into its rules.

There are certain words that you dread hearing her say. The first is *money*. She says it one evening just before her second birthday – you are walking to the supermarket, and you search for a coin to give to a busker who is playing Christmas carols. Isla give money, your baby says. Mu-nee. You dread the way it will become as concrete to her as sky and cat and gate. Mu-nee. Mu-nee.

She will come home with new phrases each time she visits her father. Granny has eyes in the *back* of her head. The new doggy is driving him *crackers*. She will learn a whole new idiom from school. Other people's phrases will ring, precocious and uncanny, in her voice: Adi had to go to time-out because he made some *poor choices*. That is CLASSIC. I'm not impressed with your behaviour. No offence. I'm just, like, having a seriously bad day.

You know that she will pick up *bad words*. You find that some of your friends moderate their language around her, and others cannot. He's such a dickhead. Excuse my French. But he is. Two older girls at after-school club will teach her to say fuck (*What is cough backwards? Ha ha*). She uses her phonics to sound out the word S-E-X, which has been written in Tipp-Ex on a climbing frame at the park. But none of these words is as incongruous in her mouth as that first bad word, jangling there: mu-nee, mu-nee.

Spurt. She is overrun with words and sounds. She stammers sometimes as the words rise too quickly for her to formulate. She pretends to speak in French and babbles like a baby again. She extemporises wild stories. She is greedy for all your words too. One night, when she is feverish in your arms in a hospital waiting room, her skin mottling, her pupils dilating, she points to a sign: What does that say? she asks. Accident and Emergency, you tell her. What is emergency? she asks. And you try to explain, and then she says: Tell me every word that you know. And as you wait for a doctor, desperate for a doctor, you list words that she might not have heard: iota, cusp, saltfish, cleft, delinquent, exuberance, incantation.

I love you, she calls out to you some nights from the depths of sleep. IloveyouIloveyouIloveyou, she sings to you when she wakes and is searching for you in the dark.

I love you too, you reply. But your words sound flat and mean.

There are tests of love in children's story books. How much do you love me, asks a winsome baby creature of its parent. *To the sky. To the moon.* Which is not enough. *To the moon and back again.* These stories remind you of the idea of impossible words. Words like God. And silence. Words that destroy what they claim to evoke. Love is an impossible word in your mouth.

You want to fill the space of the night-time with a sound that roots you together through the deep chambers of ear and brain and abdomen. You coo to her then. *There, there. I'm here. It's ok, it's ok, you're ok.* Is it wordless, what you seek? Back to that old silence, which was never really silence: the blood in your chest beating through her cheek as she lies against you; your heart's rhythm pulsing through her veins.

But this is only in the darkness. In the daytime, she is in a language beyond you already. You didn't tell me,

she says to you one morning, bright with accusation,
You didn't tell me that it's chicken *pox* not chicken
pops. You didn't tell me I was saying it wrong.

You'll learn, belatedly, about the stages of speech
development through which she has already passed:
babbling, jargon, holophrastic stage, telegraphic stage,
spurt, sentence, complexity.

You catch her speaking to herself under her breath:
I can do this, I can do this. She begins to scribble in
a small book when she is overtaken with fury at you
– I'm angry with all my sixty hearts! – and then, later,
repentant, she'll read the words she's written to you.
My mummy is a tell a liar. My mummy is the wurst.

You'll find that you cannot correct her writing, either.
Insee winsee sbider wons apon a tym got on the chrain.

Oh, but the dream language that still erupts from her.
The babble that drives her deep play still. The words
she invents at the cusp of sleep: There's a monster
called Barook that lives under my bed. Persons don't

have fur. I wish everyone in the world could live here, even the ones I don't know, so I could share shoes. I'm telling myself a joke. Self: what makes a pig fly? This day my breath made a cloud. What if the crocodile is dead from a powerscratch? You're a billy belp. I am desperately, desperately not sleepful. What is tsunami?

What is tsunami?

The crash of her words. Pouring in of world. Prodigious wash that draws her in close, and sweeps her far, far away.

Gail McConnell

Talk Through the Wall

you say you   think you feel you   might be able just   to sense the
baby bubbles   that's the feeling   bubbles on the   walls like bubbles
pressing up   against the sides   & popping at the   line the books
say they're too wee for kicks   or stretching pushes to be

felt to register inside   your skin but   but you're sure   you think you're
feeling something like their   contact something   giving shape to this
arrangement something   annotating what   this is all

happed up in   a caul & tapping   out negotiations   little one starts
wiggling the eyebrows they now   have & testing   out their joints to see
the bends   of elbows knees   & toes of waving hands   of kicking
feet of tilting   head of shifting   hips of curling   tongue of fingertips

with fingerprints already grooved therein of taking to the mouth
the thumb of testing out all texture & of placing fingers on
this fine-haired skin their covering as flexing limbs find boundary

lines know what it is to be inside to be within to grow
attached though not to me through blood & cord we make another
way to fasten each to each nightly I speak with you talk through
the wall about the day & tell you of the work I did or didn't do

& read you rhymes like London Bridge is broken down though who is
this gay lady who's rebuilding it with iron & steel with iron & steel that
bends the dance goes on returns repeats dance o'er my Lady Lea dance

o'er the three or four or five ply yarn spun out for you in air
to jump before it sweeps the ground I burble on in skipping songs
in chants that come that come & go from the bottom of the deep
blue sea sea sea with a heel a toe & a barley O

Gail McConnell

Now

after Louis MacNeice

The room was suddenly you

    and the great bay-window I pressed

palms to as a child came whippling back

    beyond the spawning factory you started in

your mother plump with eggs they counted out

    in snow and hush the embryos collateral: a key

ring compass rose revealing cardinal directions wordlessly

    happening this instantly and yet to be formed us –

paper gowns and paper hats and silver shining scales

machines beep beep and spit out sheets

scribbling to chart your heart inside the shell and out

of it into this theatre room fluorescence

with a bubbling sound for world

       whawha whawha whawha

              is come

  on the ears on the ears on the ears on the ears –

you   petal delicate pink-cheeked and damp between our hands.

Gail McConnell

Untitled / Villanelle

'I have often longed to see my mother in the doorway.' – Grace Paley
'Because having a father made me want a father.' – Sandra Newman

I have often longed to see my mother
tap-dance in a top hat like she did before he died –
having (had) a father made me want a father.

A mather / madder / mether is a measure
that keeps its shape & holds what's stored inside –
I   often   see my mother.

Mistype the word it stretches to a fother
(a cartload carries fodder, hitched outside) –
       a father made me.

You come to know the one against the other.

You measure till the meanings coincide.

I have often longed to see my father.

My mother's mother died before her daughter was a mother.

Alone, she gave me all she could provide –

(not) having a father made me want (to be) a father.

What am I to you? Mother? Father? Neither?

Like cells, names split & double, unified.

I have often longed to   mother

mother father fother mother matherfother fothermather

Gail McConnell

An Apple Seed

apple cup & shell
I say these things to you   I read them
from the   book   book   book   this is   a

book   you roll yourself to where
the sound must be   to sound to word to thing
to me the mouth that sounds out ssssssssshhhhhhhh

ell   you watch my lips to see the shell
come out   come out shell the shell
comes out & curls itself around the air

again the thing   itself is waves
of sound   for sound it is a swimming
moving to & fro   vibrating shell

the peel & rind   creaturely home   upon a time
spacetime is soft-bodied
Einstein said   *the mollusc*   we are in   a constant

flux   the quantum world stretching twisting curving
your small body to my own your hands
against my lips your fingers on my tongue

what is that sound what currency
is this what vessel for existing
sssssssshhhhhellllllll

when you were still in shell   we counted you
in days   two cells on day one   four the second day
six the third   when you were placed

inside   another room   to make
your way an apple seed   a blueberry   an ear
of corn   a coconut   the day of shelling

came & went   till two weeks   on you flexed
we were two Sauls   something like scales
something like shells   were falling

from our eyes   as out you came
you come out with a cry just like the aaaaaaahhhhhhhhhh
of apple

Malcolm Taylor

To be where I am not

You slip into the world bejewelled with your mother
and ask with half-lidded eyes for my help.
I don't know what to do with you but already it seems
I don't know what to do without you, either.
At 4am the midwife sends me home. The deer in the
headlights turns and stares and I make to stop, but she
lifts her head and is gone.
There was something in those eyes though, yours and
hers, and I can't be sure I know how to respond.
I am here yet I am not sure where that is, and it seems
you make me want to be where I am not.

From time to time you resent my arms, an ungrateful
ball of scarlet wet fury kicking out for a reason never
shared.
I must put you down and walk away, or so say all the
advisors. All the many, many advisors.
And I could do that, but today there is nobody to

step in. We hold on determinedly, you and I, exactly
neither of us knowing what to do.
I ask you where we go next but you refuse to answer.
You shake instead and the tears flow.
I no longer want to be here, because you have made
me want to be where I am not.

Later, when the place I am settles down once more and
there is calm, the contrasting pace of things stands out.
Where did it come from, this life we made, and where
is it going? Time only accelerates and I become a date
on a stopped watch a week or more old.
You shift from my orbit, little by little. You grow.
The deer again, on a slab this time and marble run.
Eyes listless, head dropped, hair longer and crimped
with pale-flecked tips.
Where would you like to be, someone asks. Not here,
not now. Thank you, not now. You made me be where
I am not, and I don't know how you did it.

Liz Berry

The Other Mothers

It's the ones just ahead who obsess me
    – risen from dark waters,
faces dazzled by rain, hair sequinned
    and cool as scales. I follow them
through playgrounds and school gates,
    their stink of river water and limes,
the salt of want tingling my gums.
    Even their names pierce me, trembling
through the tiny bones of my ears:
    Rupinder, Jess, Madeleine, Joy.
How their bodies glow and loosen
    with untouchedness.
They catch their faces in the mirror
    of the classroom window
as they wave goodbye: shocked to be back
    and singing in their skins.
Some bear a scar like an archer's bow.
    I am sick with longing, want to bite

the green apple of their days.

    When the house grows unearthly
still with napping, I peer through
    the blackout blinds, catch one
out running, silver crowns shooting up
    from the puddles, her face upturned
to the storm, lips parted
    as if calling it her animal – –

Liz Berry

Godspeed

When we fuck in sweet darkness
I leave my body behind, rising
from her as smoke rises
from the forging fire.
Godspeed, I tell her,
as we part like lovers
on the threshold.
I want to begin again,
move as the creatures
of the air do, birds, moths,
ghosts shimmering
in the empty streets,
the theremin song of the trees
as they shed their inhibitions
against the gold light.
The blood and jewelling
of the body, its grief
and burden, abandoned

like an unreadable book.
I wish I could take you with me,
but one of us must stay
behind, keep watch
upon the darkness,
our sons' warm limbs
reaching like tendrils
from their cots.

Liz Berry

Princes End

At dusk, pigeons rush to write
the last words on the page of the day
and the fodes are a poem of wings.
There, between the cut and Lost City,
among the dandelion kingdoms,
is the loft where I held her,
one afternoon of your newborn spring –
a tippler hen like a little queen
lifted from her throne of straw.
I'd never held a bird before
and my hands shook as when I first held you,
downy squab, in the hospital,
afraid of hurting you, wanting your trust.
It was Bill who showed me how
to make a cup of my palms, clasp her wings
to steady the jimmucking flight in her
and when I felt her heart –
its startling clockwork – against my fingers,

suddenly I knew her:
her porcelain egg, the grits in her throat,
her wild hours winging from clouded cities.
She was you and she was me,
the black winter of birth behind us
like a storm blown to sea,
and when I fanned her feathers to the light
to see the plumes she'd moult
I saw the ghost of the new wing
shining beneath, how I too
might become the bird you needed.

Liz Berry

Blue Heaven

Our poem which art in blue heaven,
give us this morning,
daffodils spilling Spring's song like yolk,
moss sporing on the guttering, snug
for wet-the-beds; jenny-wren and weeping birch
watching over us, our unanswered emails
and half-built Lego palaces, milk cups
and toast crumbs, photographs of us
in the nineties, drunk and so in love
we look like children.
Give us griefs and small kindnesses,
wunce apon a time in clumsy boy's hand
on the back of a phone bill,
library books and Germolene, sanitary towels
soaked with clotted rubies,
pyjamas shed beneath the bunkbeds
like adder skins, money spiders, stories,
the nights we touch in darkness

with that wild honeymilk of recognition.
Tenderise our hearts to all that is holy:
the dog and her blanket, the playgroup collage,
and forgive us our trespasses –
pulling tight the shutters on our hearts
when others are knocking,
cussing in the night when we stumble to the cot.
Teach us to love each other as the tree loves the rain,
never wasting a drop.

Rachel Bower

Flight

I build your hive
around my body,

slip you nectar,
mouth to mouth,

your stomach
heavy with gold.

I polish your wings
to mirrors,

rub copper stripes
to a gleam.

You will crawl
further, brighter

as I crumble
but when

it is finally your time

to spiral to air

do not look
down for me:

you were never mine
to lose.

Rachel Bower

Continue on Loop

We all fall down in the ring of roses.
Crushed rice cakes spill from my pocket.
Flushed, I wipe the parquet floor, keep singing,
down at the bottom of the deep blue sea,
catching fishes for our tea! A mug of milky
brew goes cold. *Atishoo, atishoo, we all jump*

up. I am sweating. *My baby is a jumping*
bean. I escape the church hall, inhale roses,
the baby on my back, crying for milk.
I kneel to steal a petal for my pocket
then regret it – he is louder now. I see
a dog, point it out hopefully, singing

the Mary had a little lamb song
as I rush to cross the street, jumping
at a car that I'd missed. I see
a mother pram pushing towards me, rosy
and serene, nothing flying from her pockets.
My breasts sting tightly, let down milk.

We just need to get home and you can have milk
I yell to the baby in my best sing-song
voice, *we'll be there soon.* I grope my pockets
for snacks and speckled frogs jumping
into pools. He arches, the wail rises,
shattering glass like the banshee. I can see

our street. Home. We are in. The neighbour sees
me pull out a breast, plug the scream with milk.
We sit, he glugs, I breathe. Swap sides, then I rise
to change him, lie him on his gym, sing
as I empty the bin, pull out wet washing, jump
a plastic king, a shepherd, a brick. I pocket

the chocolate for later. Tissue in a pocket
so the washing goes back in, *a sailor went to sea sea
sea,* feed the baby in his highchair, dab his jumper,
his chin, his shining cheeks. The milk
bottles clink when I put them out, and I sing
of green bottles, the invisible work of the rose

the falling of petals, the swell of sea, the rising
again from severed stems, and we jump up and sing
of pockets of rye, then lay close together in milk.

Ruth Charnock

three tarot cards for the new mother

You sit down, opposite a woman. She lays out a square black cloth, with gold rectangles marked out on it. She explains to you that the cards cannot predict the future, that they are not a way to escape from anything, that you should think of them as helpful provocations regarding your current situation. Every card contains an invitation, she says, if you're willing to accept it.

What do you want to talk about today? You touch your stomach, you touch your head, you touch your throat, you touch the table. She nods and hands you the deck, inviting you to draw three cards.

***

death:

I'm surprised that the floor of retail establishments across town aren't daily littered with the exhausted bodies of postnatal mothers. [Una Dinsmore-Tuli, p351]

Why should mothers, any more than anybody else, be good? We talk of a mother's suffocating love. But the one in danger of being smothered by love might not be the infant but, under the weight of such a demand, the mother. [Jacqueline Rose, p81]

***

Ah, yes, new mother [says the tarot reader, as if this were inevitable]. You will die to yourself. No-one will tell you this though there might be talk of old bodies left behind tits at your waist continents going missing in your fanny prolapses not quite being yourself...

[She gestures vaguely downwards.]

The invitation of the death card is to surrender yourself to the change that is coming, to offer your willingly neck to the executioner's knife.

Are you ready? she asks beakily, leaning across the table, taking your hand.

***

death #1:

What is this mothering that requires a complete sub-jugation of yourself. Every part of your body must now bend towards him:

crooked back from nappies nappies nappies on the bed
cricked neck from pose of loving mother watching
   baby feeding
which pram is better this one is lighter but this one
   has a deeper shelf
needle in stomach roll get better for baby
blood thud down on hospital shower floor
pop up on all fours so I can see you from behind
(there you are!)
how is mummy doing today

You take a bath, solution of tea tree and lavender swill-ing around your stitches. Watching yourself, miniature and blurry in the tap, you realise this is the first time you've done something you absolutely, absolutely can't ever get out of.

death #2:

baby sleeps in corpse pose

baby sleeps like a crucifixion or starfish

baby is dreamboobing

baby is next-to-me

baby sleeps when the baby sleeps

You drink and drink and drink. Courvoisier, 10pm at the kitchen table, a remnant from the pregnant Christmas when you posed all full and imminent by the tree. The person opposite once made your ovaries ping and swirl golden like that shirtless man holding the baby on the Athena poster. Later, you'll quietly fight in bed, over the baby. He'll get up and fall down the stairs and, because yours has never been a practical-enough house, you'll mock up a dressing for his bleeding foot made from gaffer tape and maternity pads.

[Frozen pads, peeled out that first night at home when you have entered the underworld which – who would have thunk it? – looks exactly like the house you just left, dripping blood down the stairs, ambulance outside, except the blood has gone now. You wish it was still there, a map to get back inside before you split down the middle to let him through.]

death #3:

You go to feed a friend's cat, high up on a terraced street. It's 7am but you're used to being out in the world at this time now, although it doesn't feel like the world, really, more a place you lumber round in circles until it's time for the baby to sleep again.

You park the pram behind you on the steps as you unlock the door. When you turn around it has gone and it's like the moment at the beginning of every *Casualty*; you'd be watching thinking oh don't stand behind that combine harvester and then. You are screaming and running down the hill but, even now, it's like something is dragging you back to your old life and if you just stopped or turned around there it would be, all laid out like a banquet you didn't know was yours to eat.

The pram hits a red Polo and glances off the side, coming to lie flat on the pavement. You gather up your baby. Maybe you are still screaming but so loud that everything has become quiet. He seems fine.

death #4:

You go for a floatation tank session. Your partner has been having regular floats; he comes back euphoric and reborn and you want in on that. You're doing self-care. You climb into the egg-shaped pod, and pull the cream lid down. The man has said to be naked and to turn the lights off for the full experience. You've heard that floating of this kind is supposed to give you back-to-the-womb feelings and you're excited to instantly shed the past 40 years and feel safe again. Waggling your toes and fingers in the heavily-salted water, you think: 'I am a foetus; I am yet to be born.' The piped-in music fades out, as the man has told you it would.

There you are in the black small wet, waiting for the euphoria to come.

Oh, it is not good. The panic seeps in, cold mercury, up your legs. You are becoming stone, not all lovely and fish-like. It occurs to you that you were not safe in the womb, not at all and so, if this tank is a womb-like space, then what you have actually paid for is a recreation of your perilous gestation, wherein your mother had to take anti-spasmodic drugs to stop her womb from expelling you.

I'm going to die in this floatation tank, you think, or, maybe I am already dead. Because if I'm not, then why am I not lifting up the lid, getting myself free?

***

the empress:

Dying is easy: it's living that scares me to death. [Annie Lennox]

It was better when we were
Together in one body. [Louise Glück]

***

You are Demeter! crows the woman as she taps the card. You're pushing out the Earth from your cunt! Your titmilk will make the glaciers, the rivers, a puddle in the Tesco's carpark! Your daughter will leave you over and over again, the ungrateful slut!

***

You've never been good at receiving and yet you're always asking for things, she adds casually as she extends a red claw towards the lighter. What was it that you wanted from this?

***

ooh you're blooming aren't you blooming aren't you aren't you look at your lovely thick hair

***

A gift:

When you are pregnant, your mum gives you the tarot deck that you have always known her to read with. It's a Greek myth deck, informed by Jungian psychoanalysis. As a child, you watch her from the stairs as she unfurls the silken black cloth, smoothes it down onto the carpet then, with a swift flick of her hand, arcs the cards out, face-down, for the querent to pick from. This action, the ceremony of it – the glamour! – will become your ur-image for female sovereignty. Here, at least, your mum is powerful.

You are confused, then, and not a little troubled by this gifting which feels like an abdication of some kind. Of what? Motherhood? Being a witch? She just drives down one morning, hands it over as if it's nothing. You remind her that you already own this deck – it was your first, when you were learning to read. But she doesn't seem to hear you.

Does she think you'll need this specific deck, for the journey ahead?

What kind of inheritance is this?

* * *

5 pairs of scratch mitts
2 jars of nipple rub
5 blankets, all hand-knitted
3 piggybanks

Muslin cloths, various

Buddhism for Mothers: one copy

Women's wellness essential oil

One ham and mushroom pie

One bran loaf

One spliff, labelled 'for the evenings' with a happy face
  doodle on it

Women's wellness massage oil

Two copies of *What Mothers Do*

smell of sweet fudgy baby head

little soft paw squeeze

find the nipple find the nipple ah

courtly long froglet legs

both parts of us in one skin sequence

tincture of you *need* that steak now

tincture of legitimised daysleeping

this smoothed out silky time

[how long will you be able to write about this before the memories fade you want to be unboxing and
expectant you want to be smeared in jojoba you want
him stuffed back inside so you can see him again for

the first time but this time know who he is who you are.]

*　*　*

After he was born, you thought about burying the cards. If it's too obvious to say that you were thinking about burying your mother then let that stand – everything felt correspondent in those days, everything an umbilical cord, everywhere a baby crying, every shape an outstretched need you weren't able to tessellate with, all was want want want especially you.

[You didn't though, did you?, says the reader. You're the one who went under. You know, she felt herself dying as she pushed you out. She saw that light, didn't she? And chose to stay. And you expect her to *enjoy* you, still? But you won't enjoy *her*?]

*　*　*

Am I in a cornfield?

Yes

Am I wearing a dirndl?

Yes

Do I have a crown on my head shaped like a castle to signify my ability to create safe homes?

Yes

Do I 'govern the orderly cycle of the seasons and the laws of the cosmos'?

Yes

Am I 'the Mourning Mother, who cannot relinquish her possessions and who avenges any intrusion of life's conflicts into her ordered, Eden-like world'?

Yes

Am I Demeter?

Yes

Am I Persephone?

Yes

Am I Hades?

Yes

***

Demeter's problem was that she didn't know when to give up, the tarot lady comments as she peels a hard-boiled egg. You'd think she would've been grateful for the rest. Put her feet up, maybe have a wank. Remember that she had a body once before all this making and making and bounty and making.

***

Jacqueline Rose, reading the journalist Ariel Leve's memoir of her mother, recounts how Leve would come home from school and:

... find her mother naked in bed, from where she would summon her daughter to re-create 'The Happiest Day of my Life.' Ariel [...] would be expected to undress, curl up in a foetal position against her mother's body, her mother would pretend to push her out from her vagina and she would crawl out between her legs [p106]

[Greedyguts, the tarot reader cackles, shovelling Walkers cheese and onion into her black maw].

***

Somewhere in the universe, you are always giving birth to me, a friend's daughter says to her one morning, mouth full of cornflakes.

three of cups:

There will always be something that escapes the remit of what a mother and baby can be for each other. [Jacqueline Rose, p125]

We are the makers of one another. [Sophie Lewis, p19]

***

And where were your sisters while all this was happening?, the tarot reader asks.

You touch your heart, you point to the television. You both turn to watch a crow fly past the window.

***

A friend offers to change your son's nappy and seems surprised that you are surprised. After she has gone, you weep and weep.

A friend brings him chocolate, every time.

A friend says of course she'll be part of your village, why didn't you ask.

A friend closes your bones for you, binding you tightly in Mexican scarves, rubbing the cortisol crystals from your hips.

A friend buys him a jumper with foxes on and describes early motherhood as indentured servitude.

A friend pulls out all the black smoke from your womb and holds space while you give birth to a book, a dragon's egg, a piglet, a lamb.

A friend sits down in the sea with you for an hour.

A friend tells you that she once set fire to her baby.

A friend.
A friend.

A lost friend.

Two lost friends.

A friend sees a valley between two hills at the same time as you see a circle of women standing around a fire.

A friend knows it the exact moment he is born.

A friend buys him a book about a carrot and a pea who, even though they are irrevocably different, still manage to become friends.

A friend binds her wrist with red cotton, tells you all she felt was guilt.

A friend teaches you how to breathe into the floor of your clenched womb.

They watch with you as the pram rolls down the hill, over and over again, coming every time to lay flat on its side, a card flicked out from a deck, like it was nothing.

For Flynn: somewhere in the universe, I am always giving birth to you.

Works cited:

Uma Dinsmore-Tuli (2014). *Yoni Shakti: A Woman's Guide to Power and Freedom through Yoga and Tantra*. London: YogaWords.

Louise Glück (1975). 'For My Mother' in *The House on Marshland*. New York: Ecco Press.

Annie Lennox (1992). 'Cold' from *Diva*. New York: RCA Records.

Sophie Lewis (2021). *Full Surrogacy Now: Feminism Against Family*. London: Verso.

Jacqueline Rose (2018). *Mothers: An Essay on Love and Cruelty*. London: Faber & Faber.

Juliet Sharman-Burke and Liz Green (1986). *The Mythic Tarot*. London: Rider.

Abi Curtis

September Birth

Doors opened on the terraced street
And they came out, as if to tell the weather,
Greeting you as the soft blood dried on your skin.
Messages lined the shelves
Covering the spines of great books
And storm clouds opened on the rooftops.
In the weeks after your arrival the leaves burned.
Hydrangeas turned to paper and late
Strawberries blushed, heavy on their stems.
You floated through the world in the arms of others,
Slept long dreams as if at sea,
Waking ravenous from the journey.
Your faintly-drawn eyebrow lifts in puzzlement
Or knowledge. Your skin smells of eggshells
And your breath shudders in your lungs
Then settles like seed on the breeze.
Your ears curl like conches.
You came to tell us something;

It is there with the milk at your lips,
In your eyes as they track every source of light.
It has been with you always in the darkness
Pulsing over the live wire.
You sing it out in a cry from a mouth
the shape of a broken heart.
We listen close but cannot fathom
Your new language. We will spend
The rest of our days learning it.

Abi Curtis

Ultrasound

The sonographer's jaw was set;
she didn't turn her screen.

I bit my lip and stared
at the suspended ceiling.

In the silence a few seconds
remained where I could believe

you lived. She was so sorry,
said I could see you, if I wanted.

In the static: the buds of your hands and feet,
your soft, heart-shaped head.

You'd died, she said, perhaps
a week before, and I wondered where I'd been:

choosing grapes in Sainsburys
their shiny red skins under the lights.

Or waiting at the black and white
crossing with my son (your brother)

for the green man to give us leave.
Or with my wrists deep in the washing up

the moment your heart stopped.
My body didn't know it was a living

grave, as your father wrapped his arms
around my swelling waist.

So they put me to sleep;
three beautiful ladies in scrubs.

One stroking my cheek, one counting down,
one giving me sweet drugs:

Belladonna, cherry laurel, hemlock.
So I wasn't there as they drew you out

of the liquid dark into the light;
a product of the nights we

pushed against the boundaries
of our flesh, miscalculating love.

I dreamed of bees: their vibrations,
their white houses. The glade filled

with the fuzzy song of your future name.
My eyes opened to a stranger,

a nurse with hairy hands that held
my hand as I wept.

I supposed his job was to draw me back
from that apiary of the dead.

'I lost my baby.'
'Yes. I know. I know,' he smiled and said.

Abi Curtis

On my son, falling asleep

Your tomcat face is wide, unwhiskered.
Your skull weighty as a coconut
or the globe. Your ears: shells that sing
not the sound of a shore, but laughter
and sussi, uh, tuks, babbi.
Your belly swells with cheese and blackberries,
heels of bread, stubs of potato.

Air purrs inside you, engine-bright.
Milk-white canines tip the hot gums;
you feel for mine with a sharp thumb
to know what your mouth might become,
touch the sighs, the questions.

Zipped up with toes in a bunch,
I lay you down
heavy as a marrow
fingers star-fishing for daytime things.
Wrapped in the dark.
Waiting for the strangest dreams.

Abi Curtis

Water Birth

You unfurled in the water
blue as a bog iris
still tied to me inside by
the looped telephone wire
our blood spoke on,
skin soft as the air itself

the air you took
that flushed your skin
as all the pain drained
in the egg-shaped pool.

Midwives talked softly and made notes
while you fed from me and I wrapped
myself in blood-stained sheets.

They spread the organ that I grew
out like a fan embroidered
with capillaries
to ascertain its truth.

I find that I can tie my shoes
and stretch my lungs
that your fluttering limbs are
touching the surface
not the underside of skin.

Birth is an unmaking of me
so that you might be.
Your face familiar.
Named for dexterity
for the gorgeous things that hands
might do: heal, write, hold,
make music.

I dress you in purple remembering
cloth used to be dyed by hand
coloured with crushed gems
or the soft bodies of mini beasts
the violet water streaming through
white streets
finding its way eventually
back to the sea.

Jennifer Cooke

Inside the Eye

Before you are born, we call you Pisco, we call you lobito.
You wake when we wake. You are active, a wriggler.
I swim in cold waters and you keep me warm.

I am totally unprepared for how furious I will be after
the birth. In the bedroom the baby bites my nipple
and I cry out in agony as my parents sit in the living
room, aflush with happy anticipation to meet their
first grandson. I descend the stairs step by painful
step and burst into hopeless angry tears in front of
them. Later, icy cool in the overheated house, I berate
my confused mother for coming to see us so soon in
response to my invitation to stay in the hotel I had
booked for them. I am implacable, righteously scolding:
she is wrong, she has failed me, my words thrown like
lashes.

Your infant face scrabbles at my breast and I call you my snufflepig. I am high for you, even as my body bleeds and seeps, is sore and raw.

The newly painted walls stream with condensation from the roiling beans, windows and doors closed against the winter cold. I contemplate this scene in silent rage.

You are my tiny, beautiful, little-old-man baby. My heart is breaking for you.

She holds you for hours to help and I make a lasagne and am incandescent. I cook up ways to prise you back. Breastfeeding hurts but only I can do it. I contrive excuses to do it alone.

You begin to lose your newborn hair at the front, then in the middle. We call you Olaf Scholz, we call you Rogan Josh.

There are many video calls. I am in my nightclothes, my ugly knickers thick with blood-soaked pads, trying to improve the latch, hoping to feed in better positions, full of fury.

You know what you want, and it is not your crib.
You want to sleep on us. You have not really unfurled yet.
You tuck your head under our chins, as you had under my
ribs for months, riding breach, my homunculus, soft skull
not far beneath my own.

In the middle of the night, I hear the van drive to a
stop, the clunk click of the doors, thud, thud, thud,
clunk click, then the diesel accelerate away. In the
morning, the rubbish bags bulge against a broken
cupboard, spilling someone's unwanted life across
our chilly street. I hear these drops once or twice a
week, maybe more, breastfeeding through the night,
and each time I imagine a confrontation where I pull
a gun on the dumper, make him shit himself as he
cowers from the sudden hit of industrial lights.

We encase you in a hands-up swaddle and call you
the angel of the north.

The community midwives are full of bustle but each
one issues different instructions. I am angry: there
is no continuity of care, we see a different woman

each time. My son is not gaining weight fast enough
and I am fuming that no one seems able to advise us
properly. Give him top ups, they tell us, as though
we know what that means. Pump eight times a day.
When, I think desperately. He has to have formula,
another says. But I want to breastfeed him and am
infuriated they seem intent on fattening him as fast as
possible to get us off their books and into the hands
of the health visitor, who, to this day, has still never
visited our house. I begin to keep track of nappies
and feeds, when, how many, how long, in a futile data
collection that also makes me mad. No one seems that
interested in what I record.

> *We call you Chipi Chupi. We call you hermoso.*
> *We call you cosita.*

Everyone tells you to 'sleep when your baby sleeps',
absolutely useless advice until your baby is much older
than a newborn. 'It takes a village to raise a child' is
also bullshit in those early few weeks with your first
baby. Later it is wistfully glimpsed, a distant dangle

of uninhabitable utopia for those of us with family afar. A few weeks after our babies arrive, another new mum and I confide in each other guiltily: we'd like the village currently cramming into our homes so often to fuck right off. Why can no one remember what those first eight weeks are like when you are a new parent? Their odd, suspended temporality, their relentlessness, the need I had to hold him close, our hearts newly enlarged so tight against our chests, tears leaking from our eyes, and the hormonal high water mark that makes sleep deprivation somehow a bearable knife-edge? I am bad-tempered about these stupid sayings and this universal forgetting, even now.

When you feed, you move your limbs. I call you Waggle Legs.

Yet another Saturday finds me pushing the pram around east London on my own, wrapped in warm fury and longing to be three not two, weary, with aching feet and a baby who only sleeps on the move, my partner busy elsewhere. Is there any form of childcare which is not transactional, I wonder,

squatted in my forge where I blow and mould my ire
to a dull finish.

I call you Baby Boo, a name I used to use for the older cat,
and sometimes, to my own bewilderment, still do.

My mother-in-law tried to warm the wet wipes on the
radiator. It made me cross. Why? Now, I could not tell
you. Mine was a mysterious, almost cruel reaction to
her compassion for my son. Months later, I recall this
moment and feel what she felt: poor baby, so small
and the wet wipes always cold. In those early days,
I did not have the baby blues, not at all. I had the red
mist of early motherhood. I too was being born, and
I was enraged.

We call you bebecito. We call you Pisci.
Increasingly, as you grow into your once slack skin,
we also call you by your name.

Paige Davis

This Too Will Pass

His voice came as if through thick fog, marsh.
Curtains opened, covers thrown aside,
each morning the screams since September.
Breastmilk was all he wanted, as if he
were a drunk. Needed the hair of the dog.
Begging, pleading, she had been told whining
this too will pass. He's two, he's too old
The cries are as helpless as a 2-day-old
It makes her stomach ache to make him wait.
This too will pass.

Hand on his chubby shoulder she squeezes
It feels like clay she could mould
it will dry, become hard.
Ceramic like the bones of his older brother.
When she dries up, when she stops
because this too will pass. The milk stains on bras
smelling sour, his tantrums for mummymilky and then
one day he will have his last drop.

He will roll over and fall asleep without her body to
take him, lull him into the fog of dreams.
She will cry and the feeling will overwhelm her.
This too will pass.

Janine Bradbury

Meridian

There's a photo of us straddling time;
our arms + legs outstretched; Vitruvian
parts of us spanning a line that cuts South
to Accra, then Tema before sinking
subaqua to where Drexciyan babes glide
with no longing to be part of this world.
I think of my belly, globed + marked dark
with its own longitude & you inside,
amniotic. You have mapped us a new
cartography, where to hold is to love.
And I tell you: Once, there was a great swell
& we were beached by sheer chance on this shore.
Your dumpling feet will pad my silver stretch,
waves that marked my mother & her mother.

Poem note: Drexciya is the Afrofuturist vision of the Detroit Techno
band of the same name. It tells of an underwater civilisation populated
by the children of enslaved pregnant women thrown overboard by their
captors into the Atlantic: tinyurl.com/253w83aa

Janine Bradbury

Stranger Days

'How is she doing?'
                    'She's out of this world!'
A truth I swaddle in plain sight, snug, wrapped
in the clichés for love we're fluent in.
See, they don't know that the first word you wrote
was   J
            U
                P
            I
        T
        E
        R, shaped as a question mark,
eyes-wide like ET pointing to heaven.
Green men beep at the crossing. It is time
to go home through the park, where shadow leaves
fall from the trees & spiked conkers hurtle
like comets from heavy mother branches.
Maybe I can keep you, learn from your ways.
Your civilization is so advanced.
You kiss my face. I know you came in peace.
You beam away & I am left in pieces.

Janine Bradbury

Jellyfish

while gazing at a smack of moon jellies
at the Monterey Bay Aquarium
my actual brain floats up through bone & glass
& joins them pulsing off towards blueish
apparitions   of things that used to sting
but now can soothe instead   my mother's hand
the properties of nettles   aloneness
your latch   the first one eased by amnesia
the last adaptation   i lactated
cyborg milk like legions of cyborg mums
my spare parts   cold   suspended   in Milton
come alive   this ecstasy of let-down
i don't know what natural means i wish   i
could stretch its meaning like a   jellyfish

Poem note: The Monterey Bay Aquarium streams real-time footage of
their moon jellies: www.montereybayaquarium.org/animals/live-cams/
moon-jelly-cam

Elizabeth Hogarth

Animal Body

It's time
She can feel the telltale sign dripping down her leg
the tightening in her belly like a punch.
She chews on the last of her breakfast,
her last meal for a while, and joins the herd,
shepherded into the sterile stable,
billowing partition panels to separate the animals.
A thin veil suggesting privacy, but providing none.
They can all hear her braying
as she endures wave after wave of pain.
They snap their rubber glove and insert fingers
into her taut, bucking body
and tell her it's not enough.
She makes noises that she's never heard before,
she huffs, she groans, she brays some more.
The sweat drips off her forehead, down her back
and pools at her swollen hooves.
The cockerel makes a time call
somewhere between minutes, hours or days.

It's time.
She's taken from the stable, wheeled away
toes dragging across the hard floor,
door, door, door, bright white light,
a noise somewhere between a scream and a roar.
She doesn't know what animal she is any more
only that she is a beast with a job to do.
They shout her instructions, breathe, push
and her body should know what to do,
should be able to do these simple things
only they're in charge, she has no control.
Instinct left with the blood between her legs.
She listens, she obeys, her body submits
and her child is dragged out, warm and crying.
She lies back with her baby in her arms
and pulls out her breast. The baby latches on
smearing her with blood and placenta
as her milk churns.
This animal body is not her own.
It was made to be a Mother.

Elizabeth Hogarth
Shark Tooth

A great white shark has a body
built like a blunt torpedo
and 300 serrated teeth.
My little shark has 4 teeth
and every night I summon Steve Irwin
and slip a nipple into his waiting jaws
playing Russian roulette
as to what state it will come out in,
mottled, purple, bleeding.
Those are the high stakes
when you're feeding the hungry.
A little shark with toothache
and a bite like a nail clipper.

Elizabeth Hogarth

Injured Bird

The slow-motion slip, feet in the air,
ground rushing up to meet his face.
To plant him in a bed of hard earth
and leaves just starting to brown and curl
sharpening at their edges.
He is soft and warm,
tucked in arms like an injured bird,
clinging to skin like he could slip
inside of it. It is gentle.
It is safe. He cries.
He cries as the trees sway above him,
as the clouds move across the sky,
white and wispy giving way to blue,
a sparse expanse drifting on forever.
No end, like these tears.
We leave behind the trees, the clouds,
the thirsty blue sky
and take a plastic seat

in grey halls, with the retching
of illness and pain lined up inside.
Take a number, take your turn.
and the little bird curls up tighter
in this awful, clinical place and waits.
The machine is intimidating,
looming over the butchery table
like an angry moon
but all it does is cast light
through his skin, his flesh, his bone
to make its verdict in a pale haze.
We slip past the grey walls in a daze
and break out back into the daylight.
The same long day.
He stretches out his wings,
feels the breeze through his injured fingers
and flies.

Sylvie Simonds

The bonds of love

The bonds of love
A brutal taking of magnificent spoil
And what is of this thing
You describe as continuity
And poignancy
I can see across my retina
Of Blueness and aptitude
We may think more together
About these internal states of mind
With confusion
And belatedness
But my message I say: isn't it always clear?
I often wonder about miraculous things, and magical people
And my strangeness, your sense and description of
    foreignness
Using the word repetitively; I say isn't it strange
Strange, you said that word strange a few more times today
Adrift, now and we might think it is forgotten

Alex McRae Dimsdale

Bath

The nurse dipped cotton wool into a metal basin,
carefully rubbed the chap off your lips,
wiped the flakes of dried blood
in between your toes. She washed you so gently
after they'd drawn out the cannulas
that pumped oxygen to your lungs –
after we'd all held you,
parcelled in the shawl
your grandmother brought from London
after we – me, your dad, your grandparents,
the gaunt Liberian chaplain, the stricken midwife –
had sung 'Jesus loves the little children'
from photocopied service sheets.

She asked if we had an outfit for you
but it was down the hall
and I didn't want to cause bother –
so she dressed you in white
hospital clothes, this big woman

we loved, although
we didn't know her –
Did she find it hard to be alone with us,
that last time we saw you, love?

It wasn't the first time that a couple had to leave
the hospital without their newborn.
What could they give us instead?
Here, a small white wooden box –
inside, a packet of wildflower seeds,
your wristband, little
stripy hat. A curlicued certificate
inked with your footprints. White flowers
from the youngest nurse on duty,
bought on her shift break. The name
of a psychiatrist.

Then it was just me and your dad in the darkened room.
I had been worried you'd be cold,
but you were not because she'd held you
under a warmer. The light
glowed on your coppery hair.
I saw your face directly, your closed eyes, I never

knew the colour, but oh,
I saw you clearly, you were naked, perfect,
every part of your male body
as it was meant to be –
and I saw your character in your face,
tough and forthright, I saw
years and years stretch out
then concertina back. There was so little
for me to go on, what
mistakes might I be making,
what maternal sin did I commit,
deciding who you were
for a whole life that was
already stopped before it started?

Alex McRae Dimsdale

Disaster

'An unfavourable aspect of a star or planet' [Obs.]

Your father and I flail in another galaxy.
Like all new astronauts, we adjust to darkness.
We wake at night, our shining eyes
enormous as we reach for each other.
We are many miles apart from you now, love.
For months before your birth, we tracked your purposeful
ellipse as you swung close enough
to graze us. Your perihelion
lasted twenty hours, a tranche of blinding minutes
when we held you, the heat of your small
stubborn body burning in our arms.
I tried to scorch your replica
of your father's face onto my retina.

Long ago, two months after my sixth birthday
my parents took me to the hill behind our house
to see a comet in the fog.
My mother said 'Remember this,

next time it comes back you'll be very old.'
I remember only the sharp cold,
the excitement of being up so late
with the shadowy grown-ups,
our breath like mist, not the star itself –
a smudge of something leaving
in all that cloud. Such a shame
I could not carry this memory
into the future, to tell it to my children,
also somewhere out there,
their fiery tails already directed
inexorably towards me.
All I'd carry would be disappointment
as we turned, we and the comet,
propelled from each other
into the funnels of our separate nights –

Alex McRae Dimsdale

Feeding the Baby

His hunger cries tug me awake
disoriented to find a baby
in the dark blue intimacy
of our bedroom.

Now we are home;
gone from the hospital, goodbye
night nurses in pink pyjamas,
tending their incubators
like bees.

Now, when I lift him,
there are no wires to dislodge,
nothing to be retethered.
He finds me quickly, latches on
with small contented sighs.

Now, I own him: padded bottom,
unused feet; the terrifying pulse
below his fontanelle. But this is June,
the briefest of the year's nights.

My mother says that sometimes
when she shuts her eyes
she can still feel the weight of my head
pressed into her shoulder, warm body
in the red and white striped nightie.

Even now, she says
she could close her eyes and find the other me,
the me that wasn't me, who was all hers,
solid in the blur of endless nights
when I was small enough to carry,
the word 'no' not yet growing in my mouth.

Alex McRae Dimsdale

Things I have removed from my baby's mouth

A well-chewed wad of the *Financial Times*,
wedged like putty on the roof of his mouth for days
until I saw the beige and black mass,
and panicked that it was a palate defect
the doctors must have missed.

My nipple, as I slide a cautious finger
inside the pulsing muscle of his cheek.
Sunglasses, ergonomic headphones, keys.
A rabies tag once attached to the dog's collar.

Today he's got into the groceries –
clementines puckered with teethmarks,
a raw potato slippery with spit.
Absorbed in the inspection
of a crinkly pack of kitchen sponges
he gums it, probes, and casts the thing aside,
scans around for something new,

wails as the dog's water bowl is whisked away,
the fridge door zips shut.

Why do we crave what's out of reach?
Give us secret things, new things that we can pry apart,
with unwashed sticky fingers.
Give us the cold interior of lilies,
felt-lined chess sets, violin cases, locked gardens
in leafy city squares. Give us antique
pocket watches, sealed letters, give us
swimming pools with no one in them,
flat and gin-clear.

He doesn't like the wooden blocks
I bought, imagining I'd help him build
the floating turrets of a childhood.
What toy could compare to this thrill
of the forbidden? He bites down hard
on what he wants, sharp-toothed, triumphant
till I blindly fish the car keys out.

Alex McRae Dimsdale

Covenant

Having learnt to sit,
the child's head balanced
with the perfect posture

that is a stage,
(as all such moments are,
so they say, those who've seen

the repetitious movie that is childhood
several times before
and say they know the usual endings)

he fixes his immaculate attention
on a ladder of sun leaning
through the window to the floorboards –

but he looks up when I click my fingers,
coax him by the name I've given him,
his face turning, opening like a flower

and though I hold up the phone and take his photo
anyway, it's almost painful that he looks to me,
that he trusts I will have something better

to show him than the bars of light,
better than what he'd chosen,
as, after all, I promised him I did.

Daisy Hildyard

Waste

The first pregnancy test was tangled up with all the rest of Mateo and Silvia's trash. Strands of Silvia's long dark hair, spent coffee-grounds, and the things Mateo had tossed aside – a navy-blue sock he couldn't find a partner for, a half-eaten piece of toast. The small white plastic stick had cold toast-crumbs clinging to its surfaces. On the stick there was a tiny window the size of a baby's fingernail. In the window there was a faint view of a negative sign.

Four weeks later another test arrived at the landfill site. In the same black plastic bag there were three more tests, lying at different levels with layers of rubbish between them, as though Silvia and Mateo had tested again and again each day, unable to believe that the result was complete. All of these tests were negative.

Months passed at the landfill site. Each day lorries came out from the city, through the suburbs, to deposit tonnes of matter on the dump's ragged, shifting hills of waste. Patches of grass and fibrous weeds set root on these slopes and shot up. Then something tumbled or collapsed; a small avalanche of rubbish uprooted the seedlings, scattering seeds to spring up elsewhere. Used pregnancy tests continued to arrive here, regularly, from Mateo and Silvia's flat. They came in every month, sometimes every other week. They were always negative.

Foxes, rabbits, insects, and several bird colonies lived at the dump, which was situated between a railway line and a lake. High up on a hill above this lake there was a place where a broken bucket had lodged on a shelf and formed the basis of a small, stable plateau. A pair of gulls made a nest here and the mother laid two eggs. She sat patiently on her nest. Her grey, white, black, yellow body blended into the dark mass of waste, specked with colour, that she had made home. The eggs hatched and she fed her young, her mate helped. They worked in concert, without interacting. As one arrived with food, the other departed to feed. They brought worms and insects to the nest. Occasionally there was cooked meat, spilling out of a bag, or carrion.

Meanwhile the pregnancy tests were gradually pushed apart, some tumbled to the base of the slope, others were nudged to the deep interior. Above, insects slowly crawled, birds rose and landed, polythene cracked in the breeze, the moon and sun travelled across the horizon. Below the surface the trash was warm. The old pregnancy tests were washed by waves of softer rubbish and largely ignored or forgotten by all living things. New tests came in with Mateo and Silvia's rubbish. Inside each test there was an absorbent stalk, and the stalk held fluids from a body. There was ammonia, salts, and water. There were cells in which Silvia's chromosomes floated. But all the tests were negative. The young gulls fledged. Another year came.

In spring the gulls returned to the same nest. The mother laid three eggs and sat on them, waiting. Inside Silvia and Mateo's waste there was an appointment letter from an obstetric consultant. It was crumpled up inside a length of oil-spotted kitchen-roll. By the time the chicks had fledged, a second letter had arrived at the dump. This letter, also from the obstetric clinic, stated that all test results had come back 'normal'. It had been torn into many small pieces.

For years, the gulls returned to the same nest, and at the same landfill site, pregnancy tests arrived regularly and frequently from Silvia and Mateo's flat. And then one spring the gulls did not return. That year, the pregnancy tests arrived less frequently, almost erratically. Sometimes months went by without one. Sometimes there were several, all bunched together, taken and binned in quick succession. One bag, with several used tests inside it, landed near the gull's abandoned nest and split right open. Eventually the tests stopped coming. Within the bag that the final negative test came, either Silvia or Mateo had also dropped a pair of baby shoes. There was a price sticker on one soft, unmarked sole, and a plastic tag that attached the shoes to one another at the back.

* * *

Silvia and Mateo's waste changed, with time. Over the years the bags that they used became neater and smaller, carefully tied so that the contents would not spill. They took to recycling and composting. Mateo didn't throw away clothes any more, or abandon his meals half-eaten. The long strands of Silvia's dark hair went grey.

A pair of young gulls arrived at the abandoned nest. They settled on it and made some changes. The female brought in new twigs and stalks, a few pieces of string, and nudged them into the cupped space at the centre of the nest. The father pulled fluff from his chest for the lining. The female laid three eggs. While she was sitting on them, the father disappeared. The mother continued to wait. She was a stout, quiet bird, preoccupied with purposeful inaction. In early spring, two of her eggs hatched and the third went cold.

Of the two chicks, the smaller was always weak. It died one cold morning before dawn. The mother removed this small body from the nest and dropped it in the lake. She couldn't dislodge the unhatched egg, which was heavy and smooth, and attached to the nest's slightly tacky surface. So it remained, like a stone or an alien beside its sibling, the only surviving chick. He was strong, with a small straight pink tongue and a jangly cry. The mother fed him all day and often past nightfall. The weather turned, it got warmer. The chick was doing fine.

Beside the gull's nest there was a pregnancy test. It had spilled from a split bag, years earlier. It had a negative sign in the window, clouded now. The large baby gull pecked at this pale, fish-shaped object. He took one end into his mouth and attempted to chew it. The plastic didn't give, but the capped end slid into his craw. For a few long moments, nothing happened. Then the gull tipped his head upward and the plastic inched downward and stuck. One half of the pregnancy test protruded from his mouth. The other half impaled him. He retched. His muscles pulsed around the plastic stick, but the plastic stick was stuck. Its end pierced a membrane at the back of his throat and the membrane burst. Acids, enzymes, and blood entered the gull's lungs and seeped upwards, out through his beak and his mouth. His neck was thin. When he could no longer bear the weight of the test, he laid his head down. His body barely moved after that. He lay there, blinking, for several hours, as stomach acid pervaded his bloodstream and fresh blood filled his stomach and there was nothing between the inside and the outside of him that spilled beyond his body and into his nest on the dump, soaking into the waste material that surrounded him. His mother continued to deliver food to his corpse throughout the following day, and the day after that.

Time passed. There were no more pregnancy tests from Mateo and Silvia. Their rubbish testified to the fact that they continued to drink coffee, to work part-time from home, to go camping together in early autumn. Everything shows up at the landfill site, if you give it time. The physical components of suffering or love or the experience of waiting for something, are discarded and mixed up. Used condoms from the abattoir break-room. Grape-peelings from the palace nursery. Mateo and Silvia's rubbish still arrives at the site every other week. Sometimes a browning bouquet of flowers shows up in the mouth of the bag, in there with their grey hairs, damp teabags, and empty blister-packs of pills. A flourish of late, enduring romance, or just a bit of colour to brighten up the flat. Eventually the flowers melt away, however, the spent pregnancy tests have not yet degraded. They're still there, lying in the core warmth of the landfill site. One day, archaeologists will try to make sense of them. Perhaps they had ritual meaning. Maybe they conferred protective status. They could have been ordinary household implements. Perhaps they were used for making art or music. They were love tokens or status symbols. They were technology or weapons.

Rebecca Goss

Other Mothers

'What does it mean to let go the envy?' – Sheryl Luna

I am not interested in your baby. I am not interested in your birthing story, your laboured gasps, your euphoric trip home from the hospital. I am not interested in the type of pram you chose, the sleep you're not getting or the NCT bonds that you made. I will not Like the photograph of your newborn baby in my timeline. I will not peer inside your shiny new pram and coo at what I see there, but if I do, it will take an effort so Herculean I'll turn away from you in that supermarket aisle and feel winded of my every breath. Because it is deleterious to look at you. The multiple yous, circled in parks and cafes, the spaces where I sit with my book and watch you lift your babies from their prams, smooth their unspoiled bodies upon your laps. I was fully expecting it to dissipate, the envy. I never thought it would remain so ferociously unchanged. Over time, my grief has morphed. It has raged and calmed and raged again.

It has rendered me sleepless and helpless; it has made me articulate and strong. My grief has become both companion and foe. But envy, and resentment, bitterness, spite remain as intoxicating as they have always been.

~

I want to tell you what happened to her, but that would be cruel. Women don't hurt each other like that. Yet I want to put down my book, step inside your ringfence of baby bags to explain that I stare because I am jealous. I am jealous of such normalcy. Of the staggering ordinariness of your sitting together, with happy babies, in a public space. It makes me want to hurt you. By hurt you, I mean hear me. You will clutch your babies as I lean close, and listening will be painful.

~

She was born so easily. A labour lasting only hours; no pain relief, my breathing controlled. I understood what was happening to my body; could process the pain because I knew a good thing was coming. Then her cry, my husband's voice, the holding of her. She was here, it was done. Midwives, industrious around us, everything seeming fine and soon I was in a room with my baby girl curled against my chest, reading a book of poems, my phone quivering with new blessings. I rarely think of the first thirty-six hours before she was diagnosed. All that time when I held her, changed her, imagining the stretch of our future days. My husband's voice on the phone, so eager to bring us home. Then the paediatrician's knock on the door, coming to look at her as I was gathering my things. Do you think she looks a little bit blue? Did I think my baby looked a little bit blue? No, I did not. I did not know where to look for blueness. Should I have been looking? I had no idea what she meant. But I followed her as she pushed my baby's cot to intensive care, where she was greeted by one medic, then two, three, four, five. I let my baby be surrounded, put into an incubator and I stood there. So much activity around her body, but nobody knew what to tell me. I turned my head to look at the other incubated babies my child had come to join, each with their own glittering cluster of nearby machines. The room was white, in the early afternoon, but

I recall it getting dark. I looked at people's backs, as they looked at my child. I watched people watching screens. I heard a voice say, *Look at that valve, it's all the way down there.* Someone told me to phone my husband. I was led to a desk and in the end, I could not make the call myself. I had to hand the receiver to a doctor and let a stranger tell him that there were issues of concern with his baby's health, and he needed to come to intensive care as soon as he could.

~

By this point in the story, you will be clasping your babies tighter. Not for one minute will I consider your own experiences. That you too might find yourself at the threshold of your home needing to weep and splutter because it is just too hard, this business of child-rearing. That you too have been scared and alone and I might have been wrong about you all along. But, you see, your child is one of the countless healthy children to be born since 2008. Countless. I am trying to forgive you for that.

~

So, my story will resume, and oh, what choice! Which part of her early days to focus on, to inflict. Perhaps the part where my daughter was transferred from one hospital to another in a blue light ambulance. My husband and I following in our car, dumbstruck. Or my failed attempts to breastfeed in hospital, tubes spiralling from her tiny, bandaged fists. Or the time I left my newborn baby on the ward having notified the necessary nurses of my absence. Clutching wash bag, towel, and clean clothes, in search of a private place to wash. Walking the hospital corridor thinking that if my daughter woke, I had no idea if anyone would comfort her. Finding the sickly pink walls of a hospital bathroom. A rusting metal shower and speckled mirror. The flooring worn, grey, unclean. Not wanting to put my bare feet upon it. Fashioning a bathmat from blue paper towels. Towels that would later stick to my wet feet, so drying myself became a desperate farce. Turning on the water and stepping inside the shower's dilapidated frame to cry and bleed. Forgetting I was still bleeding until naked like this, when I had to face my post-partum body. The physical effects of her birth eclipsed by being repeatedly told of her fragile life. 'Palliative' hurting a lot more than 'post-natal'. The shower becoming my secret space to howl. A place to mourn the alternative beginning. The one where I did not veer so violently off-course, did not decamp to a children's hospital but instead took her straight home to the Moses basket, the night-light, the hand-knitted cashmere blanket. Just like you took your babies home. Instead, settling myself into Ward K2 to re-text the contacts in my phone and cancel out that first joyful message from only days before. Asking people to think of her, to hope.

~

By now I have punished you enough. I should push back my chair and excuse myself. You will watch me and say nothing, your tea gone cold, your babies squirming, your fingers frantic to return to the act of cherishing. But do you see how this beginning affected my relationship with you indefinitely?

~

I will sweep over her death. I will smooth past the frantic rush around her body, and my scream. How the hands of the other mother in ICU rushed to her mouth when she saw me. How she came to find me afterwards and cried and said sorry and said sorry again. How I took her hands and told her to go back to her baby. I had another child. Born healthy. There is no reason to suspect she will do anything but outlive me. Therefore, the company of other mothers is company I still keep. Or rather it is company I both covet and reject. School playgrounds see me drenched in toxic self-pity. Standing near other mothers, working out how to interrupt a casual chat about maths homework to say *I had another child who died...* How does that conversation start? It doesn't ever start. Instead, I often stand alone, waiting for my living child to rush from the building's doors, its stuffy classroom heat still in her hair as she runs to me, grateful for her warm scalp under my palm. All around me, the milestones of her contemporaries. Medals for gymnastics, the SATs scores, the music exams passed. I continue to be jealous of these minor triumphs. That they were reached. Meeting other mothers for the first time causes my mind to spend several manic minutes assessing if I will tell of the daughter who died. If I think there is a glimmer of hope this other mother and I might get on, I fear such news will ruin things from the outset. That the news will not be received well, and I will feel guilty for spoiling things. Because there have been times, instances, small moments of disclosure, when I have regretted being so open. My utterance to another mother has been met with an insufficient response, any curiosity about me suddenly halted, everything about her wanting to retreat. I have felt foolish, shameful. Occasionally, I do tell another mother and she gets it. I mean really gets it. I cannot stress how monufuckingmental that is. She hears the words, she processes them, she asks an astute question or two, she lets me see that this will not be the only time we talk about it. I want that response from every one of you. I greedily demand it. There are easier women to befriend than me.

~

Of course, you don't see me. With your babies gurgling on your knees. There is nothing to identify me. I am a middle-aged woman, with a book. There is nothing visible to prove that I once woke and the child I stroked to sleep was no longer there for my touch. But I see you.

~

If she had lived, my daughter would be a teenager now. Mothers with prams would have shifted to my periphery vision. Instead, you stand out, and with every flap of muslin at your breast I feel punched. Furious and grudging. I know I have a capacity for kindness; a huge, abundant, generous capacity to be kind to women, but it has been sabotaged by my grief. What have I become? I go right back to the girl who was quite good at hurdles, shit at maths, excellent at spelling. I picture her, and her girlhood. See her sitting on the school field with her friends. Her grown-up life lying in wait. If I could whisper a warning in her newly pierced ear, I'd say one day your body will bend, forcing you to stop and sit on a shop floor because the sadness will mean you cannot take another step. You won't care that people are staring. You won't care about anything but the child you will lose. I'd say prize what you have: another child's fingers pressed in your hand, the consolation of her mass as you lift her from the ground. I'd say try not to be so angry. Try not to deny the other mothers their deserved maternal peace.

~

I do not want your child, I promise you. I just want your fortune. Coming out of hospital, weeks after my poorly daughter's birth, meant I could never catch up with you. While I was praying for her fractured heart you had already conducted your forensic conversations about labour. You had moved onto tales of feeding and sleeping, whilst strolling together in your newly formed group and I was so far behind, wanting to be with you, waving and drowning at the same time.

~

Caleb Klaces
The Carrier Bag Theory of Fiction

You have invited me to testify as an expert witness to this inquiry into the space debris incident of 14th July of this year. It seems your intention is to blame someone for the outcome. As chief engineer of the CZ-3B "Gaia" mission, I am here to tell you there is no one to blame.

On the contrary, CZ-3B represents, in my view, the very best of our species.

I gave a decade of my life to the rocket, and I understand its workings as a parent understands their own child. I know that it was designed in line with current regulations, and that it performed precisely as it was designed to perform. There was no malfunction and no fault in the construction.

I am proud to tell you the story of its lifecycle.

The rocket was assembled in the Glade Assembly Point from 11,826 parts, manufactured in 17 countries, using materials extracted in an estimated 12 countries.

Launching in ideal conditions, it took 157 seconds to reach the operational layer of Earth's atmosphere. This remains a record speed for the rocket class. The fuel modules detached, falling without harm into the great empty expanse of the Pacific Ocean. The remaining trunk swivelled gracefully into a smooth orbit. Orbit was maintained for a period within the expected range, during which time CZ-3B carried out its work.

It is a shame, I might just briefly add, that you have not asked me to speak about this work, because this work is truly remarkable.

Now it falls to me to clear up a misperception. At the end of a module's useful life all space agencies allow uncontrolled re-entry of spent materials into the Earth's atmosphere. As I have listened to the proceedings of this inquiry, it has been painful to hear a great deal of ignorant civilian talk about this practice.

It is true that on average once a week a hard metal object roughly the weight of an adult male polar bear falls somewhere on the Earth from space. But uncontrolled re-entry is an entirely safe practice, conducted in line with current regulations. The Earth is very large and mostly covered in water. CZ-3B's work is of incalculable value.

Upon re-entry, CZ-3B's interlockers were incinerated, as they were designed to do, splitting the trunk into three segments.

The trajectory of each segment was, of course, determined by its particular shape, size and weight. The segment that you are concerned with landed at between 8:00 and 8:10pm local time. Judging by the impact crater, it was travelling at a maximum velocity of 180m/s.

Two final remarks, if I may.

I encourage the panel to reflect on this fact: in the entire, noble history of space exploration, this is the first and only civilian fatality.

As an engineer, I encourage the rest of the industry to take note of the design of the segment in question, currently unique to CZ-3B. The man was standing only two metres from the house he was renting with his family when the segment struck. Because the object was sheer and blade-like, it fell only on him. His family were spared.

*

As Clarence approached the holiday home, he rehearsed what he intended to say...

Before you utter a word I just want to apologise for everything I shouted at you, and admit, now that I've had a walk around the village – which by the way is totally amazing, I'm almost tempted to wake up the kids and get everyone out there right now (could we do that?) – that you were right, you were right to ask if it was just that one very tiny thing that had set me off, just that single item missing from the five substantial suit-cases we brought with us, and right to point out that I was freaking out at exactly the wrong time, on our first night in this amazing place, just when you were reading a bedtime story so calmly to the older children, in their expensively rented bedroom, when I had the easier task of getting the baby ready, and I looked for the baby's sleeping bag – and yes OK the baby's sleeping bag, as a parenting prop, has gone beyond important to me, has become kind of mystical, as though by zipping the baby into a bag each night I'm protecting him against all the terrible uncertainties and threats of the world, a totally irrational, superstitious belief, and yes there *had* been a period, which I'd thought had long past, when the bag thing had got out of hand, and I'd permanently had several tabs open in the browser on my phone, each displaying a different baby sleeping bag I might buy, an upgrade on the one in current seasonal rotation, and I came to fear, deeply, that if I closed a tab someone I love might just die, suddenly, for no reason, which I know is ridiculous, but – and when I'd tipped out all five suitcases on the tiled floor and still couldn't see the bag I'd allowed myself to buy specifically for this trip, 100% organic cotton, cute palm tree pattern, shoulder-zipped, perfect for the humidity here, I admit that yes, I did just leave the baby sprawled in the sea of clothes, and did shout something at you, in your general direction, I'm not even sure what it was, but yes it was almost certainly unpleasant and unwarranted, and the last thing the kids needed before going to sleep in a strange new place, however expensive that place is to rent, and I appreciate now how calm you were as you walked over, just asking the entirely reasonable questions I mentioned earlier, and instead of listening I stormed off into the village, seized at that point by a genuine belief that I'd be able to buy a replacement baby sleeping bag here, since this is the country in which the majority of the bags are actually stitched together by hand (did you know that?), and of course there were no bags to be seen, except plastic bags of course, which are the opposite of what I was looking for, positively hazardous to a child, but then almost as soon as I was out there I looked around and I was lost, really totally clueless about my orientation, and the thing I really wanted to tell you, more than all of those tiresome explanations and apologies, is that it wasn't scary or even unsettling but just so invigorating to actually be lost somewhere, as though I'd stepped off the Earth for a moment, and suddenly I missed you all desperately, and wanted you, my treasured family, to experience this with me, and suddenly all I desired in the world was to return to the house, say everything I've just said, and get everyone up and out into the amazing village where we could all get lost together, so what do you

Sandra Simonds

Bikram Yoga

I was tired because I have a two-year-old son

so I took some NoDoz and then my heart flipped out and I

needed to relax so I went to a yoga studio.

And it was like the world was made of awkward pose. And then

life turned Caribbean

in a headstand. And then I passed

out in underwater aquamarine roses and stars. I think the

teacher said *plank*,

which meant I was a pirate in colorful spandex with

a nose ring and booty

or maybe it meant the world was ending and soon I'd

be flexible—like Zen!

I hope no one here is concerned—

the teacher said some poses take a lifetime to learn.

Sandra Simonds

Lace Clouds over House over House over House

A dirty diaper on the bathroom floor

and my toddler taking a bath, his father washing

his little back with a yellow sponge plucked from the sea.

There are submerged mountains taller

than Mount Everest in the sea. Google it.

Life and her frail salinity seem slow, saintly even, at this time

in the evening or ponderous like

the whale shark who circled the tank

at the Georgia Aquarium when we went to visit.

The children and their parents, holding hands, moving

through the engineered fish, point at
deep time's thick glass walls separating single-celled
organisms from
complexity, awe.

Sandra Simonds

Exploding Florida

Like your husband saying "Good luck with your life," a rare
    Florida orchid gets drunk on doomsday
at noon on what looks like a Middle English green, between a
    toddler in Spider-Man pajamas who jumps
from the trampoline set up on the front lawn onto a cactus
    plant and his mother, mom mama, more of her more of
        her gaga,

boo-boo, kiss-kiss, more of her scandalous life stripped to a naked
    plot twist, more fleshy Florida
where even the anesthetic used to numb, pull out the cactus
    needle is sucking and sexing.

All the pink sands of the universe funnel through this

mess of narcotic clouds

that burst like bodies, that burst their own children.

Tommy Brad

Expectant father

I expected a hard time
To be sleepless
Or not to be asleep
I expected my life to change
for the youthful worse
I never once thought
Or envisaged just how
You'd make my smile
constant inside. Wow.

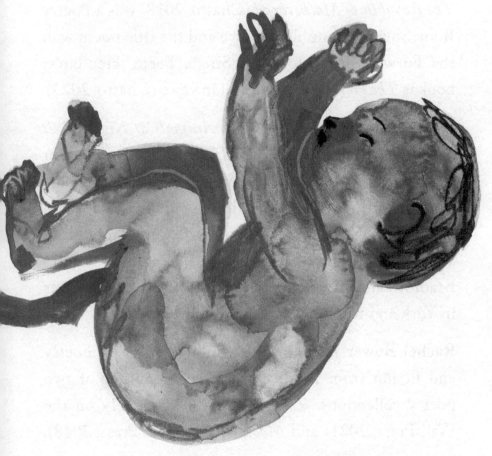

Artwork by Elīna Braslina

elinabraslina.com

AUTHOR BIOGRAPHIES:

Liz Berry's first book of poems, *Black Country* (Chatto, 2014), a 'sooty, soaring hymn to her native West Midlands'(the *Guardian*) received a Somerset Maugham Award, the Geoffrey Faber Memorial Award and the Forward Prize for Best First Collection. Liz's pamphlet *The Republic of Motherhood* (Chatto, 2018) was a Poetry Book Society Pamphlet Choice and the title poem won the Forward Prize for Best Single Poem. Her latest book is *The Home Child*, a novel in verse (Chatto, 2023).

Naomi Booth is the author of *Animals at Night, Exit Management, Sealed* and *The Lost Art of Sinking*. Her work has been listed for the *Sunday Times* EFG Short Story Award and included in the *Guardian*'s Best Fiction of the Year list. Her story 'Sour Hall' was adapted into an Audible Originals drama series. Naomi was born in Bradford and grew up in West Yorkshire. She now lives in York and teaches at Durham University.

Rachel Bower is an award-winning writer of poetry and fiction from Bradford. She is the author of two poetry collections: *These Mothers of Gods* (Fly on the Wall Press, 2021) and *Moon Milk* (Valley Press, 2018).

She is also the author of a non-fiction book on literary letters (Palgrave, 2017). Rachel's poems and stories have been widely published in literary magazines, including *The London Magazine, The White Review, Magma* and *Stand*. Rachel won The London Magazine Short Story Prize 2019/20 and the W&A Short Story Competition 2020. She is currently editing an anthology with Simon Armitage (Faber & Faber, 2023).

Tommy Brad was born 1979 in Nottingham and raised by a devoted mum and influential brother. He was socially shaped in Newark, and before having children travelled and worked globally. He settled in York and now has two children.

Janine Bradbury teaches at the University of York where she is a Senior Lecturer in Contemporary Writing and Culture. She has been a repeat guest on BBC Radio 4 and her writing has been published by the Guardian, Bloomsbury, Palgrave, and Routledge. Her poems appear in *Black Lines: A Journal of Black British Writing, Oxford Poetry* and *Magma*. Janine was a recipient of a 2020 Poetry London Mentoring Prize, and she was a finalist for the 2022 Aurora Prize for Writing.

Ruth Charnock is a writer, researcher, creative mentor and storyworker. She is the editor of *Joni Mitchell: New Critical Readings* (Bloomsbury, 2019) and makes work about mothering, tarot, feminism, affect, sex and music. Her next piece, 'Witching the Institution', a collaborative piece with Dr Karen Schaller, is forthcoming with Duke U.P.

Jennifer Cooke is a London-based writer and Reader in Contemporary Literature and Theory at Loughborough University. Her academic books include the BACLS Best Monograph prizewinner *Contemporary Feminist Life-Writing: The New Audacity* (Cambridge University Press, 2020), the double award-winning edited collection *The New Feminist Literary Studies* (CUP, 2020), and the edited volume *Scenes of Intimacy: Reading, Writing and Theorizing Contemporary Literature* (Bloomsbury Academic, 2013). Her first monograph was *Legacies of Plague in Literature, Theory, and Film* (Palgrave, 2009). She has published two poetry collections: *Apocalypse Dreams* (Sad Press, 2015) and **Not Suitable for Domestic Sublimation* (Contraband Books, 2010), has had poetry and prose published widely online and in print, and given readings in some exciting places such as Paris,

Berlin, San Francisco, New York, Edinburgh, and Santiago. She wrote a novel during lockdown which she naively and incorrectly assumed she could edit during maternity leave.

Abi Curtis is Professor of Creative Writing at York St John University. She is the author of two poetry collections, *Unexpected Weather* and *The Glass Delusion* (Salt) and a novel, *Water & Glass* (Cloud Lodge). She has had stories placed in the Bridport Prize, Fish Prize and Alpine Fellowship Prize and has been the recipient of an Eric Gregory Award and a Somerset Maugham Award.

Paige Davis is a Developmental Psychologist at York St John University and a fellow of the British Academy. Her work on parenthood encompasses play and creativity. She has evaluated a socially prescribed play programme continuing to build an evidence base for Theatre Hullabaloo in Darlington. She is also a breastfeeding peer supporter, and researches transition to parenthood. Her other research is on imaginary companions and cognitive development.

Rebecca Goss is a poet, tutor and mentor living in Suffolk. Her first full-length collection, *The Anatomy* *of Structures*, was published by Flambard Press in 2010. Her second collection, *Her Birth*, (Carcanet/Northern House, 2013) was shortlisted for the 2013 Forward Prize for Best Collection, won the Poetry category in the East Anglian Book Awards 2013, and in 2015 was shortlisted for the Warwick Prize for Writing and the Portico Prize for Literature. Rebecca's third full-length collection, *Girl*, was published with Carcanet/Northern House in 2019 and shortlisted for the East Anglian Book Awards 2019. She is winner of the Sylvia Plath Prize 2022. She has an MA in Creative Writing from Cardiff University and a PhD by Publication from the University of East Anglia. Her next collection, *Latch,* will be published with Carcanet in May 2023.

Daisy Hildyard is author of two novels – *Emergency* (Fitzcarraldo, 2022) and *Hunters in the Snow* (Jonathan Cape, 2013) – and one work of nonfiction, *The Second Body* (Fitzcarraldo, 2017). Her writing has received awards including a '5 under 35' honorarium (National Book Awards, USA) and a Somerset Maugham Award (Society of Authors, UK). She lives in York.

Elizabeth Hogarth was the young poet laureate of Middlesbrough and has a selection of poetry published in anthologies. She attended York St John University where she completed her degree in Comparative Media. She currently works at the University of York and has two boys aged one and four.

Caleb Klaces is the author of a novel, *Fatherhood* (Prototype, 2019), which won a Northern Writers Award and was longlisted for the Republic of Consciousness Prize, and two poetry collections, *Away From Me* (Prototype, 2021) and *Bottled Air* (Eyewear, 2013). He teaches at York Centre for Writing, York St John University.

Gail McConnell is from Belfast. She is interested in the living and the dead, violence, creatureliness, queerness and the possibilities and politics of language and form. Gail is the author of *The Sun is Open* (Penned in the Margins, 2021), *Northern Irish Poetry and Theology* (Palgrave, 2014) and two poetry pamphlets: *Fothermather* (Ink Sweat and Tears, 2019) and *Fourteen* (Green Bottle Press, 2018). With Conor Garrett, Gail has made two arts features based on her poetry for BBC Radio 4: *Fothermather* and *The Open Box*. Gail is Reader in English at Queen's University Belfast.

Alex McRae Dimsdale is Director of Communications at a foreign policy think tank in Washington DC. She won an Eric Gregory Award in 2009 and has had poems published in *The Florida Review, The Manhattan Review, Poet Lore* and *Gargoyle* in the US, and in *The Poetry Review, The North, Magma* and *Cast* (an anthology of young British poets edited by Simon Armitage) in the UK. Her poems have been nominated for a Pushcart Prize. She has an MFA in Poetry from Vermont College of Fine Arts.

Sandra Simonds is the author of eight books of poetry, most recently *Triptychs* (Wave Books, 2022) and *Atopia* (Wesleyan University Press, 2019). She is an Associate Professor of English at Thomas University in Thomasville, Georgia and currently a Visiting Professor of English at Bennington College in Bennington, Vermont.

Sylvie Simonds is a psychotherapist and parent-infant therapist specialising in pregnancy and parenthood. She works for the NHS and in private practice and provides consulting on subjects such as infant mental health, the perinatal period and attachment.

She is passionate about supporting parents and babies in the early years.

Malcolm Taylor is a security and intelligence profess-ional who spent 20 years working for the UK Foreign and Commonwealth Office and now works in online safety for children. Malcolm has written for fun for most of his life and was inspired by the recent arrival of two children to explore his emotions this way. He lives in York with his family and continues to write whenever he can. His long-term aim, perhaps his dream, is to be able to stop work and write professionally.

PERMISSIONS:

'Talk Through the Wall', 'Now', 'Untitled / Villanelle', and 'An Apple Seed' by Gail McConnell were first published by Ink Sweat and Tears, London, 2019. Thank you to the publisher and author for permission to reproduce these poems.

'Continue on a Loop' by Rachel Bower was first published in *Magma* 74 (2019), then in *These Mothers of Gods* (Fly on the Wall Press, 2021). Thank you to the publisher and author for permission to reproduce this poem.

'Bikram Yoga', 'Lace Clouds over House over House over House' and 'Exploding Florida' by Sandra Simonds were first published by Bloof Books, New Jersey, 2014. Thank you to the publisher and author for permission to reproduce these poems.

THANKS:

This book has been published in association with the York Centre for Writing, York St John University.

ABOUT THE EMMA PRESS

small press, big dreams

ᏣᏞᏃᎧ

The Emma Press is an independent publishing house based in the Jewellery Quarter, Birmingham, UK. It was founded in 2012 by Emma Dai'an Wright and specialises in poetry, short fiction and children's books.

The Emma Press has been shortlisted for the Michael Marks Award for Poetry Pamphlet Publishers in 2014, 2015, 2016, 2018 and 2020, winning in 2016. *Moon Juice*, a poetry collection by Kate Wakeling for children aged 8+, won the 2017 CLiPPA.

In 2020 The Emma Press received funding from Arts Council England's

Elevate programme, developed to
enhance the diversity of the arts and
cultural sector by strengthening the
resilience of diverse-led
organisations.

The Emma Press is passionate about
publishing literature which is welcoming
and accessible. Visit our website and find
out more about our books here:

Website: theemmapress.com
Facebook @theemmapress
Twitter @theemmapress
Instagram @theemmapress

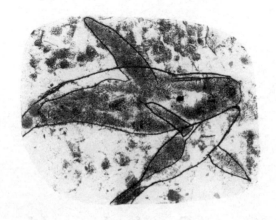

One Day at the Taiwan Land Bank Dinosaur Museum

Elīna Eihmane

This is a picture book for everyone, framed as a bedtime story (and love letter) to the author's son. It follows the events of the little boy's birth, and his mother's struggle with her new role. In stunningly raw writing that cuts straight to the heart, Eihmane tells a story about love and where love comes from.

The book is beautifully illustrated by the author, in dark blues and reds, with expressive, blotchy artwork.

PAPERBACK ISBN 978-1-912915-66-8

PRICE £10.00

ALSO FROM THE EMMA PRESS

How Kyoto Breaks Your Heart

Florentyna Leow

20-something and uncertain about her future, Florentyna is exhilarated when an old acquaintance offers her an opportunity for work and cohabitation in a little house in the hills of Kyoto.

Florentyna begins a new job as a tour guide, taking tourists on elaborate and expensive trips around Kyoto's cultural hotspots. Meanwhile, her relationship with her new companion develops an intensity as they live and work together.

How Kyoto Breaks Your Heart is a collection about the ways in which heartbreak can fill a place and make it impossible to stay.

PAPERBACK ISBN 978-1-915628-00-8

PRICE £8.99

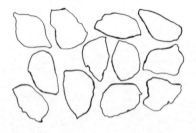

Tiny Moons

Nina Mingya Powles

Tiny Moons is a collection of essays about food and belonging. Nina Mingya Powles journeys between Wellington, Kota Kinabalu and Shanghai, tracing the constants in her life: eating and cooking, and the dishes that have come to define her.

Through childhood snacks, family feasts, Shanghai street food and student dinners, she attempts to find a way back towards her Chinese-Malaysian heritage.

'Meditative reflections on family, solitude, and belonging, intertwined with mouthwatering descriptions of noodles, dumplings, and sesame pancakes.' *Book Riot*

'Funny, compact and beautifully written.'
New Statesman

PAPERBACK ISBN 978-1-912915-34-7